Bible Sticks
An Unlikely Calling

Ron Vance

WestBow Press books may be ordered through booksellers or by contacting:

WestBow Press
A Division of Thomas Nelson & Zondervan
1663 Liberty Drive
Bloomington, IN 47403
www.westbowpress.com
1 (866) 928-1240

ISBN: 978-1-5127-4085-1 (sc)
ISBN: 978-1-5127-4084-4 (e)

Library of Congress Control Number: 2016907461

Print information available on the last page.

WestBow Press rev. date: 09/02/2016

CONTENTS

BIBLE STICKS

Two of my favorite verses are found in Colossians chapter three. The first is verse 17: "And whatever you do…." I love the way it starts out. "And whatever you do, whether in word or deed, do it all in the name of the Lord Jesus, giving thanks to God the Father through him." In other words, whatever you do, do something that will bring glory and honor to God the Father and His Son Jesus Christ. The second verse, found in verse 23, starts out the same way! "Whatever you do, work at it with all your heart, as working for the Lord, not for men." In other words, whatever you do, do your very best because you are doing this for the Lord, and the Lord deserves nothing but the very best! So whenever I do anything, I do it to bring glory and honor to God, and I do my very best for Him. I have discovered that when I do this, He will take it beyond anything I can ever imagine. I would like to share with you one way He has done this in my life.

I am the associate minister at the Western Hills Church of Christ, located in Cincinnati, Ohio. I am mainly in charge of the youth and education, but I do some work in missions and outreach. It is a great church, and I have been with that church since June 1987. Many of the kids there have grown up with me being the only youth minister they have known. The ministry with Western Hills Church has been a great inspiration to my life.

In 1988, I was asked to be the dean for a week of Wilderness Camp at Woodland Lakes Christian Camp in Amelia, Ohio. In Wilderness Camp people sleep in tents, cook all meals over the campfire, do a lot of hiking, swimming, canoeing, rock climbing, basically any kind of outdoor activity. With all the hiking we did, I thought, *I need a good walking stick*. So I picked up a stick off the ground and used it for hiking. Well, as the week went on, I tried carving in the stick. Using my old pocket knife, I carved the name of the camp in the stick. I thought that would take me all week, but I was able to finish it in a couple of days. I then carved the dates of the camp in the stick, as well as everyone's name who came that week. It was a small group of eleven. I was very proud of that stick, the first stick I ever carved.

If I could do that with an old knife and an old piece of wood off the ground, I wondered what I could do if I started out with a really sharp knife and a nice piece of wood. Off to the hardware store I went. I bought an X-acto® knife with a variety of blades and a dowel rod three feet long and 1¼" in diameter.

It took me several months, but I carved a stick with a variety of designs. It started out with a little guy on the top. He is funny looking and has "89" on his shirt because that is the year I carved him. The kids from my church said I put "89" on his shirt because that is what I will look like when I am 89 years old.

Some of the other designs I carved on the stick were checkers, squiggly things (because they did not shape up to what they were supposed to be), baskets, rings, swirly carvings, bricks and my name. I showed it to everyone, especially the people at my church. A very close friend of mine, Stan, looked at it, and all he could say was, "What are you going to do with it?" I couldn't believe it, no compliment, nothing but "What are you going to do with it?" I answered, "When I turn 89 and I look like the funny man on top, I will use it to walk with." But I was thinking, *When I turn 89, I will use it to hit you over the head.* Well, Stan's question was the motivation I needed. I decided to carve something that I could use for a real purpose.

I am always trying creative ways of teaching the young people at our church. They might remember it a little longer, if I could carve something in a stick.

My cousin Mary had her wedding at the Kenwood Christian Church (Disciples) earlier that year. I remembered banners hanging around the sanctuary. Each banner had the name of one of the twelve apostles, plus a symbol representing that apostle. That memory inspired me to carve a stick using the same idea.

I bought a 3' x 1¼" dowel rod. After I measured it, making sure I had enough room for all twelve apostles, I started carving. The title was first. I started with a ball at the top with a strap coming down from it. I used a wood-burning tool to make the strap look leathery, and then I carved in the title *The 12 Apostles*.

I could not find two identical lists of the apostles. The lists of the apostles are found in four places in the New Testament: Matthew 10:2-4; Mark 3:16-19; Luke 6:14-16; and Acts 1:13. There are two Simons, two Jameses and two Judases. You have Simon Peter and Simon the Zealot; James the brother of John and James the son of Alphaeus (also known as James the Less); and Judas son of James (also known as Thaddaeus) and Judas Iscariot.

Here is the list I used: Peter, Andrew, James, John, Philip, Thomas, Bartholomew, Matthew, Thaddaeus, James the Less, Simon, and Judas. I also included an image under each name that illustrated something about the apostle's life. We read about many of the apostles in the gospels, but for some of them, we have only their names. My research uncovered traditions about how they were martyred for their faith.

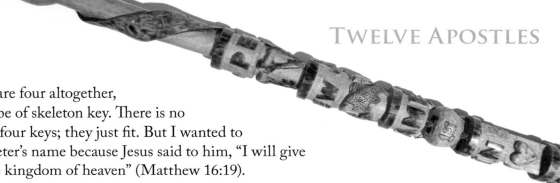

Peter: keys. There are four altogether, each a different type of skeleton key. There is no reason for carving four keys; they just fit. But I wanted to have keys under Peter's name because Jesus said to him, "I will give you the keys of the kingdom of heaven" (Matthew 16:19).

Andrew: three fish. They are all identical. I'm not sure what kind they are, just fish. Andrew was a fisherman (Matthew 4:18-20). After he met Jesus, he became a fisher of men. It was Andrew who brought to Jesus the boy who had the five loaves and two fish when Jesus fed the 5000 (John 6:8-9).

James: two swords piercing a ball that says "1st Martyr." James was the first of the twelve apostles to die for his faith (Acts 12:1-2).

John: three hearts, each a little different. John was known as the "beloved" apostle. Five times, John describes himself in the gospel as "the disciple whom Jesus loved" (John 13:23; 19:26; 20:2; 21:7,20). Love is a major theme in the first epistle he wrote (1 John 3:11-4:21).

Philip: a chain. Tradition states he was hanged by a chain until he died. Many think the chain looks like a snake and wonder if Philip was a snake handler. I don't think so!

Thomas: two hands, one pointing to the nail print in the other. Thomas became known as the "doubting" Thomas because he said that he would not believe Jesus rose from the grave unless he could put his finger into the nail print in Jesus' hand (John 20:24-29). One of the boys from my church sat in front of me for three hours straight without moving, so that I could get the hands carved just right.

Bartholomew: a crown. We don't know very much about Bartholomew from the New Testament, but his name indicates he was from a royal family, Tolomeo of Egypt.

Matthew: a scroll with a quill because he wrote the first book of the New Testament. A bag of money with a stack of coins was also included because he was a tax collector before he met Jesus.

Thaddeus: ten arrows. We don't read much about him, but tradition states that he was shot through with a bunch of arrows when he died for his faith. Again, many think the arrows look more like missiles or rockets. What can I say? It's one of my first carvings.

James the Less: two saws. Tradition says his body was "sawn asunder" when he was martyred for his faith.

Simon: a sword and a scroll. Simon was the Zealot, and a Zealot was one who defended the law. The law is represented by a scroll.

Judas: a bag with coins spilling out. Judas Iscariot betrayed Jesus for thirty silver coins (Matthew 26:14-16).

The stick took me about three months to carve. I started in the spring and finished it before summer arrived. I used a wood-burning tool to darken the names, rings, and images. I also put my initials "RDV" on the bottom of the stick with the year I carved it, 1989. The initials were made by an attachment I ordered for my wood-burning tool.

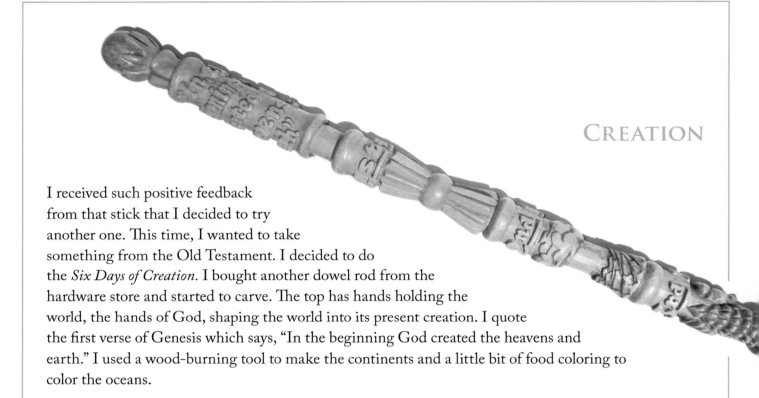

I received such positive feedback from that stick that I decided to try another one. This time, I wanted to take something from the Old Testament. I decided to do the *Six Days of Creation*. I bought another dowel rod from the hardware store and started to carve. The top has hands holding the world, the hands of God, shaping the world into its present creation. I quote the first verse of Genesis which says, "In the beginning God created the heavens and earth." I used a wood-burning tool to make the continents and a little bit of food coloring to color the oceans.

Why food coloring? I was at the wilderness camp that summer and again carved a stick with the names of all the kids who came. One of the activities we did that year was war with squirt guns. To make it look more realistic, I put red food coloring in the water. When a person got shot, it looked like they were actually bleeding. I got red food coloring on the stick I was carving, and it would not come out. I tried washing it out and rubbing it out, but it would not come out. The only way to remove it was to sand it out or to cut it out. So I decided that if I ever wanted to stain the wood with colors that would not come out, I would use food coloring! That's what I did on this stick.

First Day: God created light. I used yellow on the wood after carving it.

Second Day: God created the water and the sky with clouds. I used blue to represent that.

Third Day: God created the land and the plants. I used green to show that day.

Fourth Day: God created the sun, moon, and stars. I used black to show the space.

Fifth Day: God created the birds and the fish. I used red to show those animals.

Sixth Day: God created the land animals and man. Adam looks more like a ghost, but he is in there. I used brown to show those animals.

I closed the bottom of the stick with the *Seventh Day* saying, "God rested and it was good." This stick also took me about three months to carve during the fall of 1989. The Six Days of Creation are found in Genesis 1.

This brings me to my third
Bible Stick. I saw in a publication
an illustration of the Ten Commandments.
I decided that would be a good stick to carve, with a
picture for each commandment. When the commandments were
first given to Moses, they were not written on paper but carved in stone.
To help remember that, I found a spray paint that looks like blue stone granite. The
top of the stick looks like a stone pillar with ivy growing. The title is carved into the pillar. I
then used Roman numerals to separate the commandments, each one painted like stone. Most of the
commandments were rather simple ideas. I shortened the wording to make sure they would fit.

The First (I) Commandment: *Have no other gods.* The picture is of a little boy bowing down before the cross.

The Second (II) Commandment: *Have no Idols.* I tried to use the same little boy in each illustration. He is bowing down to an idol, illustrated by the many idols that you find in America today: a ball bat and football (sports), a diamond ring (wealth), a home (possessions).

The Third (III) Commandment: *Don't Misuse God's Name.* The boy is standing with his hand covering his mouth as if he had just said something he should not have said.

The Fourth (IV) Commandment: *Remember the Sabbath.* I have the little boy walking to church. I know, the church was not around until New Testament times, and we don't remember the Sabbath (Saturday) but we worship on the first day of the week. But I believe the Lord still wants us to set aside one day for him.

The Fifth (V) Commandment: *Honor Your Parents.* This one took me a while to come up with a good picture. I decided to have a little boy mowing his parents' lawn. I thought it would show obedience. My parents were always making me mow the lawn while I was growing up. We had a riding mower, so I didn't mind helping out.

The Sixth (VI) Commandment: *Do Not Kill.* The boy is holding a smoking gun in his hand as if he had just fired it.

The Seventh (VII) Commandment: *Don't Commit Adultery.* This was my most challenging commandment to illustrate, but I came up with a great idea that was appropriate for all ages. I have the boy contemplating two hearts that are interlocked. Everyone wants to know what kind of picture I carved for this commandment. Wow, I squeaked by with a clever idea.

The Eighth (VIII) Commandment: *Do Not Steal.* The boy is walking out of a bank with a bag of money in his hand and a mask over his face.

The Ninth (IX) Commandment: *Do Not Lie.* This picture shows the boy standing in front of a broken window. A ball is lying on the floor, and the boy's shoulders are shrugged, as if he is saying, "I don't know what happened."

The Tenth (X) Commandment: *Do Not Covet.* The boy is standing in front of a sports car, wishing he owned it. My sports car is not very sporty looking. It looks similar to an old Chevette I once owned.

The ten sections with the commandments are stained with a darker brown. I did not like the color of the natural wood; "Ramin" is a light yellow hard wood. The paint on the top pillar keeps chipping off. The letters were dark blue, but now most have the natural wood color exposing the letters in the title. I began repainting each letter, but now I leave them as they are. I think it gives the stick more character. This stick took me a year to carve. I finished it in the fall of 1990. The Ten Commandments can be found in Exodus 20.

My next stick came from the New
Testament. I decided to put *The Armor
of God* on a Bible Stick. I saw a drawing of a
Roman soldier in a Bible lesson book, and that's when
I got the idea of using that for my next theme. I started at the
top of the stick with a Roman soldier wearing the full armor, painted
with silver paint. I used a six-sided carving that looks like the head of a bolt to
separate each section on the stick.

The title under the soldier is carved in two areas, cut as spirals, intertwined with each other. The first
spiral says, "The Armor of God;" the second spiral gives the passage where it can be found, "Ephesians
6:14-17."

The first thing everyone notices about this stick is that it's in a clear plastic tube. Just a couple days after I
finished carving the stick, one of the boys from my church was looking at it (well, more than just looking
at it). His name is Travis. He was about 14 years old at the time. He was in another room when all of a
sudden, I heard a crack! I walked in, and he handed the stick to me in two pieces. It was totally broken in
two. The break happened at the spiraling title. I could not believe it! He explained that all he was doing
was tossing it up in the air like a twirling baton, and when it hit the ground, it broke. I always wondered
what I would do if anyone would ever break any of these sticks. How would I react? Well, that boy is still
living today! I was very good. I did not yell, punch, or vow to get even. I just gathered up the pieces and,
using good old Elmer's glue, put it together again. The problem was that when I went anywhere to show
the Bible Sticks, this Armor of God stick was being broken. My home minister from Wilmington, Ohio,
Art Merkle, gave me a catalog that sold plastics and told me I could probably find a protective tube for

this stick. That's what I did, and the stick has never been broken since. Under the title, the six pieces of armor are carved individually. On the back side, I identify how they are described in the Bible.

Belt of Truth: I tried to match the armor pieces as closely as possible to the full armor the soldier is wearing at the top. I used a wood stain to color the leather straps that hang below the belt.

Breastplate of Righteousness: I used wood stain to color the leather straps over the shoulders.

Shoes of Peace: I took the liberty to reword this one to fit the same pattern as before. In Ephesians, we read, "and with your feet fitted with the readiness that comes from the gospel of peace." I shortened it quite a bit.

Shield of Faith: The design on the shield is just a simple design, nothing significant.

Helmet of Salvation: Red food coloring was used to paint the comb of the helmet.

Sword of the Spirit: It is also described as the Word of God. I have a sword laying across a scroll representing the Word of God. I think it is kind of interesting that someone once suggested what they thought was the real reason I have this stick in a plastic tube. They pointed out that it was a double illustration. Just as the passage teaches we need to protect ourselves from Satan, the stick needs that extra protection from all the people who handle it. So it is in a plastic tube as an illustration of that protection. I finished the stick in November 1991. It took me about a year to carve.

We have a deaf
ministry at the Western Hills
Church of Christ that started in 1989,
with 25 – 30 deaf people coming every week. Rod
Burke is the minister. In the Spring of 1992, I was ready to
begin my next stick. I chose the *Fruit of the Spirit* found in Galatians
5:22, and I illustrated how to express each one in sign language. I began with
a variety of fruit at the top for the title. The fruit included an apple, a banana, a pear, and
an orange. I then separated each section on the stick with a carving that looks like a basket weave.
It's kind of interesting, but in the NIV Bible, the first three fruit are all one-syllable words, the next
three are two-syllable words, and the last three are all three-syllable words.

1) *Love*: I allowed myself a small square to squeeze the letters in; therefore, I had to be very creative with each one. Sign love by simply crossing your heart with your arms.

2) *Joy*: Sign joy by first of all, having a big smile on your face. Then you pat your hands on your chest in an upward motion, as if bringing that joy out of your body.

3) *Peace*: Most think you would say peace by simply holding up two fingers, but sign peace by holding your hands together as if you are praying and then sliding them apart in a turning motion.

4) *Patience*: Sign patience by putting your thumb on your bottom lip, moving it in a downward motion. I squeezed the word *patience* in its small area by dividing it into two lines.

5) *Kindness*: Sign kindness by taking one hand and going around the other, as if wrapping it with a cloth bandage. This shows kindness.

6) *Goodness*: Sign goodness by placing one hand on your chin and bringing it down to the other hand, keeping both hands flat and palms up.

7) *Faithfulness*: Sign faithfulness by making the letter "F" with both hands and bring one hand down from the forehead to the other below. It is the first of the three-syllable words. Therefore, I used three lines to squeeze the word in its square.

8) *Gentleness*: Sign gentleness by gently rubbing the top of your hand in a twirling motion.

9) *Self-Control*: Sign self-control by first pointing to yourself, then hold both hands in front of you as if holding on to the reigns of a horse and buggy, pulling them back and forth.

I used a wood-burning tool to create the designs in sign language and used food coloring to stain the words. This stick took me about one year to carve. I finished it in the Fall of 1992.

I went back to the Old Testament
for my next stick. I decided to list on
one stick *The Twelve Sons of Israel*. Before God
changed his name, Israel was Jacob. Jacob is a very
fascinating person to me, because he had a twin brother, Esau. I
have always been very interested in twins, because I have a twin brother.
My identical brother's name is Jon. We still look very much alike today and have
many similar interests. He is in the ministry also. We get along and look forward to any
times we are able to get together, unlike Jacob and his twin brother. They did not get along.

Jacob was always pulling cruel pranks on his brother; he finally had to flee for his life. He went to his mother's hometown. While there, he met a beautiful girl by the name of Rachel. He fell in love with Rachel and decided he wanted to marry her. He approached Rachel's father, Laban, and asked if he could marry her. Laban was thrilled with the idea but explained that first he would have to work for him seven years. Rachel was very beautiful, and Jacob loved her very much, so he was willing to do that.

After seven years came the wedding day. The bride wore a veil over her face. After the wedding was over, Jacob threw back the veil, and you know what? He did not marry Rachel; he married Rachel's older sister, Leah! Jacob probably let out a scream and searched for Laban to find out what happened. Laban explained that he could not marry off his youngest daughter until his oldest daughter was married. Now that Leah, his oldest daughter, was married, Jacob was free to marry Rachel. But first he would have to agree to work for Laban for another seven years!

Again, Jacob loved Rachel very much, so he agreed to do that. Now we find Jacob with two wives. He loved Rachel the most, but it was Leah who was able to have children. Rachel was barren. So Leah became the mother of Jacob's first four sons: Reuben, Simeon, Levi and Judah. Rachel became very jealous, so she came up with a plan. She had a maidservant named Bilhah. She thought, *If I give my maidservant to my husband, then when she has a child, it will be as if it were my child.* So Bilhah became the mother of Jacob's next two sons: Dan and Naphtali.

Leah thought this was not fair. She had a maidservant, also! So the third mother comes into the story. Zilpah became the mother of Gad and Asher. Leah, the first wife, had two more sons: Issachar and Zebulun. Finally, Rachel, the wife Jacob loved the most, the one who had not been able to have children, had two sons: Joseph and Benjamin. That's why Jacob loved Joseph the most and he became the favorite.

On this stick is a lot of information. First, I have the four mothers listed at the top. It is supposed to look like a leather strap, and the strap lines up with their sons. I tried to use letters that looked like the Hebrew alphabet, so some of the names have to be studied to be understood. The twelve sons are listed in the order of their birth, from the oldest to the youngest. Along the strap is a map to show where their tribe was located once they arrived in the promised land. Each map has three bodies of water: the Sea of Galilee, the Jordan River, and the Dead Sea. The highlighted area is where the tribe was located. Finally, before their father died, he gave each son a blessing. The image of the blessing is carved underneath each name. The story of Jacob's wives and sons is found in Genesis 29-30. The blessings are found in Genesis 49. Listed below are the sons, their mothers, and the blessings.

Sons of Israel	The Mother	The Blessing
1. Reuben	Leah	Turbulent Waters
2. Simeon	Leah	Swords
3. Levi	Leah	Sacrificial Altar
4. Judah	Leah	Lion
5. Dan	Bilhah	Serpent
6. Naphtali	Bilhah	Deer
7. Gad	Zilpah	Raiders
8. Asher	Zilpah	Food for the Rich
9. Issachar	Leah	Donkey
10. Zebulun	Leah	Ships
11. Joseph	Rachel	Coat of many Colors
12. Benjamin	Rachel	Wolf

For two of the sons, I did not carve in the same blessing that was mentioned in the Bible. For Levi, I carved an altar, representing the fact that Levi's family became the priests of the temple. In Genesis 49, Simeon and Levi share the same blessing. I did not carve the blessing for Joseph, either. He was blessed with a fruitful branch. I carved in the coat of many colors. In putting this stick together, I learned so many interesting things about the tribes. For example, only one tribe is land locked. It does not border any body of water at all. Which tribe is it? Zebulun, the tribe that was blessed with ships! That is priceless! Israel did have one daughter. Her name was Dinah. She was born to Leah after Zebulun was born. I finished this stick in the fall of 1993. It took me about a year to carve. This was my last stick to be carved out of Ramin, just a plain dowel rod from the hardware store.

OLD TESTAMENT CHAIN

Someone once told me they heard it is possible to carve a chain from a stick. I thought there was no way, with the way the links are connected. Well, I took a stick and started experimenting. The first chain I tried was on top of a stick I carved when a group from our church went to Canada the summer of 1991. I had the right idea but could not get the links to separate. Kate Deuitch, a missionary in Toronto, explained that I needed to allow more space where the links were connected so that I could carve that wood out of there.

In 1994, I tried it again, starting with a four-foot dowel. I came up with a chain with over 40 links, counting the hook I had at the top. It took me a year to carve that. After it was finished, I began to wonder what I could do with it. I realized there were 39 books in the Old Testament, so I could put a different book on each link. So I called it the *Old Testament Chain*. Not only did I write the names of the books, but I also included one word to describe each book and listed how many chapters are in each book. It is filled with a lot of information.

I studied and researched to come up with the perfect word to describe each book. I did not want to repeat any word, so I had to be very precise when I decided what to use. Listed below are the names of the 39 Old Testament books, the words I used to describe them, and how many chapters are in each book. I used a wood-burning tool to write the information on the chain.

Name of O.T. Book	One-Word Description	Number of Chapters
Genesis	Beginning	50
Exodus	Deliverance	40
Leviticus	Holiness	27
Numbers	Journey	36
Deuteronomy	Obedience	34
Joshua	Conquest	24
Judges	Oppression	21
Ruth	Loyalty	4
1 Samuel	Organization	31
2 Samuel	Kingdom	24
1 Kings	Division	22
2 Kings	Captivity	25
1 Chronicles	Reign	29
2 Chronicles	History	36
Ezra	Restoring	10
Nehemiah	Rebuilding	13
Esther	Providence	10
Job	Patience	42
Psalms	Praise	150
Proverbs	Wisdom	31
Ecclesiastes	Meaningless	12
Song of Solomon	Affection	8
Isaiah	Salvation	66
Jeremiah	Bondage	52
Lamentations	Weeping	5
Ezekiel	Sovereignty	48
Daniel	Visions	12

Hosea	Adultery	14
Joel	Repentance	3
Amos	Burden	9
Obadiah	Doom	1
Jonah	Mercy	4
Micah	Messiah	7
Nahum	Destruction	3
Habakkuk	Invasion	3
Zephaniah	Judgment	3
Haggai	Promises	2
Zechariah	Hope	14
Malachi	Offering	4

I found a very creative way to display the chain. I continued to twist it until it could not be twisted anymore and then hooked the ends. It looks very complicated when I display it that way. I finished the chain in the fall of 1994. It took me about a year to carve.

Since I made an Old Testament Chain, my next project was a *New Testament Chain*. For this chain, I planned from the beginning what it would be. Since there are only 27 books, I used a 3' dowel. It simply says "27" at the very top. This time, I carved in the names of the N.T. books, not just using a wood-burning tool. I wanted it to look a little different from the O.T. chain, so I did not sand it down, and I also put a stain on the finished chain. It has the same information as the O.T. chain. Each link has the name of the book, one word to describe the book, and how many chapters are in that book. Again, I did not want to repeat any of the words used in the O.T., so I had to do some extensive research. Listed below is the information that can be found in the N.T. chain.

Name of N.T. Book	One-Word Description	Number of Chapters
Matthew	Fulfillment	28
Mark	Immediately	16
Luke	Narrative	24
John	Believe	21
Acts	Mission	28
Romans	Righteousness	16
1 Corinthians	Corrections	16
2 Corinthians	Apostleship	13
Galatians	Liberty	6
Ephesians	Unity	6
Philippians	Rejoice	4
Colossians	Glory	4
1 Thessalonians	Resurrection	5
2 Thessalonians	Idleness	3
1 Timothy	Exhortation	6
2 Timothy	Encouragement	4
Titus	Doctrine	3
Philemon	Forgiveness	1
Hebrews	Superior	13
James	Works	5
1 Peter	Suffering	5
2 Peter	Warnings	3
1 John	Love	5
2 John	Truth	1
3 John	Hospitality	1
Jude	Persevere	1
Revelation	Prophecies	22

I discovered an amazing thing when I was finished carving the chain; it grew about 7 inches. The dowel started out as a 3' dowel, but when placed next to another 3' dowel, it was much longer. When carving the links, they started out very close together, but stretched out as they were being carved. I finished the chain in the fall of 1995.

Everyone wanted to know how I was able to make a chain out of a stick, so I finally made a small sample piece to show the steps. I started with a foot-long dowel, 1¼" in diameter. The first thing you do is carve four grooves, the length of the stick. If you would look from the top to the bottom, it would look like a plus "+" sign. Then you notch it on opposite sides and round your notches up; you will see your links begin to appear. The first cut is to cut between your links. Then you cut inside the links. I call this the "H" pattern. Finally, you separate the links so that they are moving freely. I could not get my knife into that area, so I made my own tool. I used a curtain hook. It has a sharp point to it and is made of metal. I attached a handle to it and began to pick at that wood. I picked and picked and picked. And then I picked some more. After a while, I put some pressure on the links, listening for the crack. If I didn't hear it, I picked some more. Finally, I picked enough wood out of there that I heard the crack. Then I took my X-acto® knife and finished the link. There are six moves that each link needs to be able to make before you go to your next link. That is how you can make a chain!

I found
a dowel shop in
the Western Hills area of
Cincinnati, just a few miles from
where I live, Midwest Dowel. The shop has
since moved to Harrison, Ohio, and changed its name to
Atlas Dowel. They make dowels out of a variety of woods. I bought
a 3' dowel of cherry. I decided to put on this stick *The Ten Plagues of Egypt*.
In order for Moses to convince Pharaoh to let the Israelites leave Egypt, God brought
on all these punishments or plagues. Those ten plagues are on this stick. They can be found in
Exodus 7-12. The letters I used for this stick are reversed, emphasizing the area between the letters. The
idea came from a drawing of Jesus' name. At first glance, all that is seen are symbols that look rather
foreign. But then Jesus' name appears.

Three little pillars separate each plague. It was something new I had never done before. For fun, I videotaped
the progress, filming one second every five minutes. With time lapse, I was able to show a large amount
of carving in just a few minutes. It took me several weeks to complete that phase of the stick. At the top,
I have the title. Egyptian symbols are also illustrated: a pyramid, Pharaoh, and different Egyptian letters.

1) *Water 2 Blood*: I have a picture of a water pitcher being poured into the river and turning to blood
(Exodus 7:14-25).

2) *Frogs*: I carved three different frogs, all in jumping motion. People could not walk around barefoot
without squishing frogs between their toes (Exodus 8:1-15).

3) *Gnats*: In this picture gnats are coming out of the sand. (Exodus 8:16-19.)

4) *Flies*: Four flies are carved in the stick. I used a wood-burning tool to finish the flies. They are life-sized (Exodus 8:20-32).

5) *Death of the Livestock*: A pile of dead animals, including a cow, a horse, and a sheep on its back, are carved (Exodus 9:1-7).

6) *Boils*: I have carved a leg and an arm. They are covered with sores on their skin (Exodus 9:8-12).

7) *Hail*: A storm cloud with lightning and hail is carved for this plague (Exodus 9:18-35).

8) *Locust*: Locusts were everywhere. They came in to eat up the crops destroyed by the hail. This picture has a locust crawling on a branch with a leaf (Exodus 10:1-20).

9) *Darkness*: It took me a while to decide how to illustrate darkness out of wood. I decided to go with the idea of open eyes with a black background. I used six pairs of eyes, all a little different (Exodus 10:21-29).

10) *Death of the Firstborn*: A house is carved with the blood of a lamb over the doorframe. The mist from the death angel is seen floating at the base of the house. In order to protect their firstborn, God commanded each family to place lamb's blood over the doorframe. This was the final plague; even the firstborn of Pharaoh died. Pharaoh commanded that all the Israelites leave Egypt immediately (Exodus 11-12). I finished this Bible Stick in 1996. It took me about one year to carve.

I went back
to that same dowel
shop, and this time I bought a
dowel of walnut. The New Testament
was the source for my next Bible Stick. I
chose the *Seven Churches of Asia*, found in the book of
Revelation. When you read these seven letters written to the seven
churches of Asia, Jesus starts out each letter with a different description
about Himself. That is the image that I chose for each church (Revelation 2 & 3).

1) *Ephesus*: "These are the words of him who holds the seven stars in his right hand and walks among the seven golden lampstands" (Revelation 2:1). For this letter, I carved seven different stars. They all have a different shape and design.

2) *Smyrna*: "These are the words of him who is the First and the Last, who died and came to life again" (Revelation 2:8). For this letter, I have two images of Christ. The first is a carving of Christ on the cross; then on the other side, I have a carving of the risen Lord.

3) *Pergamum*: "These are the words of him who has the sharp, double-edged sword" (Revelation 2:12). I started by carving four pillars leaving a section of wood on the inside. From the wood on the inside, I then carved a two-edged sword.

4) *Thyatira*: "These are the words of the Son of God, whose eyes are like a blazing fire and whose feet are like burnished brass" (Revelation 2:18). For this letter, I carved a set of eye glasses with blazing fire in the eyes. I also carved a pair of hard work shoes, representing the feet of bronze.

5) *Sardis*: "These are the words of him who holds the seven spirits of God and the seven stars" (Revelation 3:1). How does one carve a spirit out of wood? I decided to go with the idea of lightning bolts. So for this letter, I have seven lightning bolts coming out of a clenched fist. While carving, I discovered that this part of the stick was too thin, right where the lightning bolts were coming out of the fist. It was as thin as a pencil. It actually cracked on me while carving. It did not totally break in half but did crack and was wobbling back and forth. Elmer's glue seemed to take care of the problem.

6) *Philadelphia*: "These are the words of him who is holy and true, who holds the key of David" (Revelation 3:7). For this letter, I carved a box with a key carved inside the box. On one side, I have a keyhole, and on the other side, I have the Star of David.

7) *Laodicea*: "These are the words of the Amen, the faithful and true witness, the ruler of God's creation" (Revelation 3:14). For this last carving, I have the King sitting on the throne with the world in his hands, representing all of creation. The word "Amen" is carved in the back of the throne.

I used a gold trim on this stick, making a nice contrast against the dark walnut. Also, I wanted to use a gold trim because we are told what heaven will be like, with the streets of gold. I carved golden balls to separate each letter. I finished this stick in the fall of 1997. This stick also took about one year to carve.

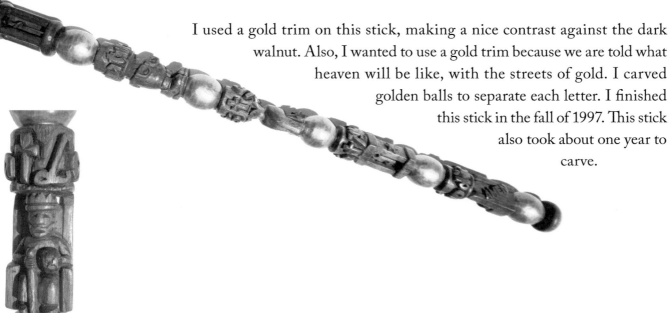

I was ready to carve my next
Bible Stick. I decided to make one with *The
Humorous Teachings of Jesus*. Jesus was always using funny
stories when he taught the disciples. They make us laugh or bring
a smile to our faces. That is what I used for this stick. I decided to carve
this stick out of oak. I love the grain, so I knew it would be a beautiful stick. The first
thing I carved was the dividing sections between each passage.

At the very top, I have the title. Beside the letters, I carved a little scroll with a smiley face on it and a quill. Now I was ready for the first passage. I chose nine passages to use in this stick. The criteria: they had to be funny, and they had to be easy to carve.

1) *Pearls to Pigs*: (Matthew 6:7). I chose this as the first one because I grew up on a pig farm in Wilmington, Ohio. It is stupid to throw anything of value to the pigs.

People always ask me, "What do you do if you make a mistake?" If you are drawing with a pencil and you make a mistake, just take your eraser, erase the mistake, and then continue on. If you are painting a picture and you make a mistake, just paint over what you did wrong then continue on. If you are carving and you make a mistake, there is not a whole lot you can do. You cannot just cut it out and put something in its place. It will be very obvious that something is not right.

Well, after I carved in the passage, Matthew 6:7, I looked it up in my Bible to make sure it was correct. You know what? Matthew 6:7 says absolutely nothing about pigs or pearls. Oh no! What did I do? I looked it up in my Bible again. It is not found in Matthew 6:7 but in Matthew 7:6. I accidentally switched those two numbers around. I could not believe it. I thought I had ruined the stick. But I had already put way too much work in it to throw it away. I decided to carve a double arrow above the 6 & 7, indicating the need to switch those two numbers around, in order to locate this passage in the Bible. I carved a picture of a pig standing on his hind legs, proudly showing off the string of pearls he is wearing.

2) *Camel Thru a Needle's Eye*: (Mark 11:25). We are familiar with the passage where it says that it's easier for a camel to go through the eye of a needle than for a rich man to get into heaven. Again, after I carved in the passage, I looked it up to make sure it was correct. You know what? I did it again! Mark 11:25 says absolutely nothing about camels or needles' eyes. I could not believe it! What is going on here? I looked at the paper I had typed. It did not say Mark 11:25. It said Mark 10:25. Why I put an 11 and not a 10, I have no clue to this day. So if you look closely, under the 11, I carved a "-1."

I debated whether I should make a mistake on the rest of the passages as well so that they would all be uniform. But I decided I should not intentionally mess up, so the rest of the passages are all correct. To me, it is God's way of making this stick even more humorous than what I had originally planned. I then carved in a picture of a camel trying to squeeze his way through a small needle's eye. He got stuck between the two humps on his back, unable to move forward or backward.

3) *Clean the Inside*: (Matthew 23:25). Jesus was always telling the Pharisees that they needed to clean what's inside and not be so concerned with what is on the outside. Jesus used a cup for this illustration. I carved a picture of a little boy proudly displaying a cup in his hand. It is clean and shiny on the outside, but if you look inside the cup, you will see it filled with dirt, crud, and all sorts of disgusting things.

4) *Blind Leadin' the Blind*: (Luke 6:39). If you are a blind person, the last person you want leading you around is another blind person. Who knows where you will end up going? I carved a picture of two blind guys; one is leading the other. They are both wearing sunglasses to make them look blind. They are about to walk off a cliff. The kids from my church say it looks more like they are on a surfboard. I guess the same point comes across with that idea, too.

5) *Wolves in Sheep's Skin*: (Matthew 7:15). The passage teaches us that you are not going to look innocent simply by throwing a sheepskin on your back if you are a ferocious wolf. I have carved here an ugly wolf with snarling teeth and a sheepskin over his head and neck.

6) *Log in Your Eye*: (Luke 6:41). How can you pick the speck of dust out of your brother's eye when you have a huge log coming out of your own eye? I carved a picture of a boy with a large wooden plank coming out of his eye.

7) *I Asked for a Fish*: (Luke 11:11). Jesus taught that God the Father is a very loving Father, and He would never play cruel tricks on us. If we ask for a fish, He will give us a fish. He would not decide to give us a snake instead. So in this carving, I have a picture of a little boy screaming that he asked for a fish. Instead, he was given a snake, and the snake wraps around his entire body.

8) *Candle Under Your Bed*: (Mark 4:21). We are not to hide what God has given us. If we do, it will be as if we are trying to hide a lighted candle under our bed. And we all know what will happen if we do that,

the entire bed will catch on fire. So I have carved here a picture of a bed on fire with a candle under it.

9) *Swallow a What!*: (Matthew 23:24). The passage says we strain the gnat but swallow a camel. I did not want to carve another camel since I had carved one earlier. So I have a picture of a boy with his mouth opened as wide as it would go, ready to swallow whatever is coming his way.

There was no certain order that I carved these teachings. And it's kind of interesting that most of these teachings can be found in the book of Matthew. But I chose a different book whenever possible. And another interesting point is that none of these passages is found in the book of John.

This stick took me about two years to carve. Part of the reason is the mistakes I made. I became very frustrated and would put it up for long periods of time, not doing any carving at all. The other reason is that I moved from my apartment to a home in 1998. It took me a while to find a comfortable place to carve in my new home. And of course, this stick was carved out of oak, an extremely hard wood.

CHRISTMAS STICK

The next stick I carved is one of
my favorites. It is unique in several ways.
First of all, it is a Christmas Stick. Everything
that you would see in a nativity or a manger scene is what
you will find in this stick. But what truly makes it unique is it is
all in Spanish.

Why Spanish? Back in 1990, I took my first mission trip to Mexico. I have been taking
a group to Mexico every year since then. We have developed a great relationship with many
Mexicans and other Spanish-speaking people because of that. In 2001, we started a Latino Ministry
with the Western Hills Church of Christ. We have about 25 –30 Latinos who come to our church every
Sunday. They meet in a room of our building, conducting the entire service in Spanish.

The other thing that makes this stick unique is the fact that each item is carved inside a cage. Most of my
carvings so far would be considered relief carvings, just carved on the surface of the wood. But this stick
shows each image in true form.

The wood I used for this stick is called Poplar. It is considered a hard wood, but it was much easier to carve
than most hard woods. Therefore, I was able to carve this stick as desired. Poplar is not the most attractive
wood, kind of yellow in color. Therefore I used a couple different stains. I stained part of the stick with
a dark walnut stain, where I carved in the Spanish words. I stained the pillars in the cage with a reddish
cherry wood stain. The image for each section is left in the natural poplar color. It starts out at the very
top simply by saying, "*Feliz Navidad.*" *Feliz Navidad* means "Merry Christmas."

The first item carved is a star. The word for star in Spanish is *Estrella*. We read in Matthew 2:2 where the wise men say, "We saw His star in the east." For each image carved, I made sure that something in the item reached to the top and bottom, to give it a little more stability. I did not want the image to break loose. For the star, I have the rays coming off the star. It was challenging to cut the wood from inside the rays.

The next image is an angel. The word for angel in Spanish is *Ángel*. It is spelled the same, but pronounced a little differently. An angel appeared to the shepherds in Luke 2:10 and said, "Do not be afraid. I bring you good news of great joy that will be for all the people." The wings of the angel reach to the top to give it stability. I wanted to carve a halo on top of the angel's head. But when I first carved it, it simply looked like a plate balancing on top of the angel's head. One of the most challenging parts of the stick was to carve the middle out of that plate, and make it look like a halo. It is a very difficult area to reach. The angel is wearing a halo!

Next, I have a shepherd. The Spanish word for shepherd is *Pastores*. Luke 2:8 says, "And there were shepherds living out in the fields nearby, keeping watch over their flocks at night." I have a shepherd carved inside the cage. He is holding a staff with a hook on top. The staff reaches the top to give the image greater security.

The next image I have carved is the baby Jesus. *Jesús* in Spanish is spelled the same, but pronounced a little differently. Matthew 1:25 says, "She gave birth to a son. And he gave him the name Jesus." Of course, Jesus is the focus of this Bible Stick. I wanted to put him in a manger. In order to stay with the same scale as the other figures, the manger would only come up half way in the cage. So I put a wall behind it, and carved a star in the wall.

The next image is Mary, the mother of Jesus. Mary in Spanish is *Maria*. Luke 2:5 says, "Mary, who was engaged to him, and was with child." I wanted Mary kneeling down, so again, staying with scale, I needed support to reach the top. I put a stable beam behind her to reach the top.

Next, I have Joseph. The Spanish word for Joseph is *José*. Luke 2:16 says, "So they hurried off and found Mary and Joseph, and the baby, who was lying in the manger." Joseph is standing with a staff in his hand, and the staff reaches the top. This staff does not have a hook.

The next image is a sheep. The Spanish word for sheep is *Oveja*. Luke 2:8 tells us that the shepherds kept watch over the flock by night. Sheep are not very big either, so I debated what to do to reach the top. I decided to place a palm tree in the cage to give the image more stability.

The other animal is a camel. The Spanish word for camel is *Camillo*. We don't have camels mentioned in the Christmas story, but most nativity scenes include camels because the wise men supposedly rode in on them. The camel is tall enough to reach the top of the cage, so I did not have to carve anything else in with him.

The last image carved is a Wiseman. The Spanish word for a Wiseman is *Reyes Magos*. Matthew 2:1 says, "After Jesus was born in Bethlehem in Judea, during the time of King Herod, Magi from the east came to Jerusalem." This Wiseman is holding up his gift he brought to the baby Jesus. The gift reaches the top of the cage. This stick took me a little over a year to carve. I did most of the carving in the year 2000.

If you carved a Christmas Stick,
what would your next stick be? An
Easter Stick. I call it *The Final Week of Christ*. It
is carved out of cherry. The unique thing about this stick
is that it has a strap or ribbon that stretches the entire length
of the stick, covering parts of the carvings. But the way I carved the
different scenes, you can still tell what is underneath the strap. I chose eight
different events that took place during that final week. Each scene is labeled; then the
images are carved.

1) *The Triumphal Entry*: (John 12:12-19). This took place when Jesus first entered Jerusalem. Jesus is riding on a donkey, and the crowds are waving the palm branches. Jesus is entering the gates of Jerusalem.

2) *The Last Supper*: (John 13:1-38). This event took place the night before Jesus was crucified. He is in the upper room with His disciples. I carved a smaller table with Jesus and two of His disciples.

3) *Garden of Gethsemane*: (Matthew 26:36-46). After the Last Supper, Jesus took His disciples to the Garden to pray. I have Jesus kneeling down to pray, resting His arms on a huge rock. While in the Garden praying, Judas betrayed Jesus with a kiss, and Jesus was arrested.

4) *The Trial*: (Luke 23:1-25). Here, Jesus is standing before Pilate, or it could be Herod. Jesus stood trial before both. There is nothing that determines which one it really was. All the false witnesses came and told their lies about Jesus.

5) *The Crucifixion*: (John 19:16-30). After they could find nothing that he was guilty of, they allowed the people to choose Jesus' punishment: crucifixion. I have pictured three crosses, with Jesus on the middle cross, the thieves on the two outside crosses.

6) *The Burial*: (Matthew 27:57-66). They took Jesus' body and buried it in a tomb and sealed it with a stone. Two men are carrying the body of Christ on a stretcher approaching the tomb.

7) *The Resurrection*: (Luke 24:1-12). Three days later, Jesus rose from the grave. Jesus is standing outside the empty tomb. The rays from the body of Jesus reflect His glory.

8) *The Ascension*: (Matthew 28:16-20). This actually did not take place during that final week, but forty days later. It is an important event that took place at the end of Christ's life here on this earth. Jesus is pictured rising to the sky through the clouds.

Originally, the strap was going to be a natural wood color, but I had trouble seeing the images underneath the strap. So I decided to use a wood-burning tool on the strap. It gave it a leathery look, but it was much easier to depict the letters and images underneath. This stick took me about one year to carve. I was able to finish most of this stick in 2001.

I went back to the wood shop and
bought a 3' mahogany dowel. I always
heard that mahogany was a great carving wood,
but I always assumed it was very hard. It was not only
one of the easier woods to carve, but it is beautiful! It can chip
and split, so one has to be very careful.

I decided to carve on this stick the *Judges of Israel*. I will explain the crosses I learned
to carve in a couple of chapters, but it is a principle I learned from carving crosses that I
used in this stick. This stick will have moving parts! When the idea came to me (I give credit to
God), it was perfect! I was so excited about this idea.

I chose seven of the Judges of Israel, found in the book of Judges. There are thirteen Judges altogether.
The last Judge is listed in the book of 1 Samuel. I chose the seven who are most familiar. I will include the
entire list of judges at the end of this chapter.

For this stick, I asked a question about each of the Judges listed. Then after a person reads the question, he
can lift up the lid, and it will reveal the answer underneath. There is probably a proper term for this type
of carving, but I will call it a hinge.

After I figured it out, I saw how much space each would take, and I was ready to carve the mahogany
dowel. It is kind of interesting that I had room for only seven judges on this stick, which is how many I
had chosen. I started at the very top with the title. I tried to make it look like the letters were attached to
a Roman style column that you would see in front of a courthouse.

1) *Who was the First Judge? Othniel*: (Judges 1 & 3). Othniel was the nephew of Caleb. Earlier, Caleb promised to give his daughter to whoever would take the city of Debir. Othniel rose to the challenge and therefore married Caleb's daughter. Later, when Israel was oppressed by Mesopotamia, God raised up Othniel to deliver Israel. Othniel is holding up one finger, indicating that he was the first judge.

2) *Which Judge Was Left-Handed? Ehud*: (Judges 3:15-30). Ehud took advantage of the fact that he was left-handed in judging Israel. One day, when he went to visit his oppressor, Eglon, Ehud hid a dagger inside his clothing that only a left-handed man could easily retrieve. While Eglon was in the inner chamber, Ehud thrust the dagger into Eglon's belly. Ehud is pictured holding a dagger in his left hand, above his head.

3) *Which Judge Was a Woman? Deborah*: (Judges 4 & 5). Deborah is the only woman judge found in this list. She delivered Israel from Sisera with the help of another woman, Jael. Jael invited Sisera into her tent so that he could rest. While he was sleeping, Jael took a tent peg and drove it through his temple. He died immediately. Deborah is pictured standing with a shield in her hand.

4) *Which Judge Blew A Trumpet? Gideon*: (Judges 6-8). There are so many great stories in the life of Gideon, but I will focus on the most familiar. After the Midianites attacked Israel, Gideon blew the trumpet and called together 32,000 men of Israel to fight. God said there were too many. He told Gideon to send home any who were afraid. 22,000 men went home. God said 10,000 men was still too many. He narrowed it down to 300 men by testing how they drank water. Through God's instructions, Gideon gave each man a trumpet, a pitcher, and a torch. They were able defeat the Midianite army with these unconventional weapons and a lot of faith. Gideon is pictured blowing a ram's horn type trumpet.

5) *What Judge Sacrificed His Daughter? Jephthah*: (Judges 11-12). Wanting to ensure victory over Ammon, Jephthah made a vow to God that whatever came out of his house first would be offered up to God as a sacrifice. When he arrived home after winning the battle, he probably thought it would be his dog running out to him; instead, it was his daughter. He fulfilled his vow. Jephthah is pictured standing next to his daughter.

6) *Who was the Strong Judge? Samson*: (Judges 13-16). Samson has many great stories, but the most familiar is the one with Delilah. Samson was chosen by God to deliver Israel. He was given great strength as long as he did not cut his hair. The Philistines were oppressing Israel at this time. Samson's weakness was beautiful women. When Samson was falling in love with Delilah, who was a Philistine woman, she pleaded with him to share the secret of his strength. After deceiving her several times, he finally broke down and told Delilah that if his hair was cut, he would be weak like every other man. While he was sleeping, they cut his hair and captured him. The Philistines loved to display their captive. After time, his hair finally began to grow back. While being displayed at a big gathering of Philistines, Samson was able to bring the building down, killing 3,000 Philistines. The carved picture is Samson with long hair, showing off his muscles.

7) *Who was the Final Judge? Samuel*: (I Samuel 1-16). The story of Samuel begins with his mother, Hannah, who was not able to have children. She prayed to God that if He would bless her with a son, she would dedicate him to the Lord. After Samuel was born and weaned, he was given to the Lord to be raised in the House of God. Samuel began to reign as judge at a very young age. He acted as a priest and prophet, also. Samuel was the last of the judges because Israel wanted a king to rule over them. He anointed Saul as their first King. Samuel is waving his hand in the carving. I was not sure what to carve here, so I decided to have him waving goodbye since he was the last judge.

The entire list of the Judges of Israel is Othniel, Ehud, Shamgar, Deborah, Gideon, (next came Abimelech, but he was self appointed and wicked, so I do not include him as part of the thirteen), Tola, Jair, Jephthah, Ibzan, Elon, Abdon, Samson, and Samuel.

For the Judges of Israel stick, I stained the moving parts a darker color so that they would stand out, but the stick is all one piece of wood. It took me several years to carve it. I finished it early in the spring of 2005, but most of the carving was done in 2004.

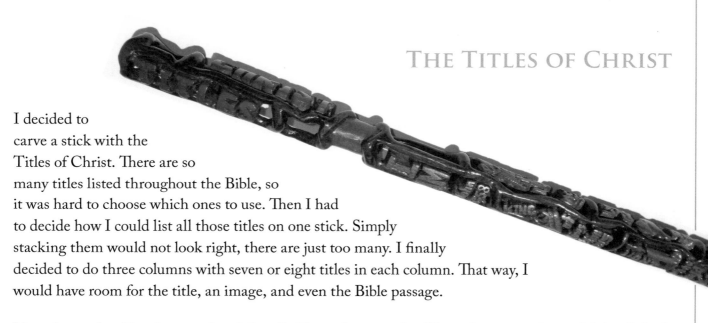

I decided to
carve a stick with the
Titles of Christ. There are so
many titles listed throughout the Bible, so
it was hard to choose which ones to use. Then I had
to decide how I could list all those titles on one stick. Simply
stacking them would not look right, there are just too many. I finally
decided to do three columns with seven or eight titles in each column. That way, I
would have room for the title, an image, and even the Bible passage.

I bought another 3' mahogany dowel. I really like mahogany a lot. Not only is it very beautiful, but I think it is one of the easier woods to carve. But one still needs to be very careful because it can split, break, or splinter. I found that out the hard way. After I worked on this stick for about 10 months, it got dropped and did break into two pieces. I was about halfway done carving it. Where it broke, most of the wood had been removed. I glued it back together, but every time I went to carve on the stick, it would break again. After another year and a half, I finally put a small wooden peg inside the stick to give it a little more strength.

This Bible Stick is made to look like a cluster of entangled vines, twisted together to hold the different titles. It does include a lot of fine detail. Because it is hollowed out and has a lot of detail and because it was broken, this stick took me forever to carve. I spent three years working on it. If I had to guess, maybe even 200 hours of carving. That is the most time I have spent on any stick carved.

People have asked me if there is any order to the titles. There is not, but I did lead off with "I Am," because that title shows His connection with God and demonstrates His eternal qualities. And towards the end of the stick, I close with "Amen," "Messiah," and "Resurrection and Life," because they better illustrate the close of His ministry here on earth.

Most of the images used to illustrate each title are simple and self-explanatory. But a few of the images are fun or need a little explanation. For example, to describe Jesus as the Rock, I was going to put a stone under that title, but when one of the young people from church suggested a guitar, I decided to go with that. For the Bread of Life, I have a loaf of bread with a chunk removed to look like someone took a bite out of it. For the Prince of Peace, I have a hand with two fingers sticking up, representing a way a lot of people express peace. Listed below are the twenty-two titles with the Bible passage and the image for each title.

Title	Passage	Image
I Am	John 8:58	"I AM"
Creator	John 1:3	The World
Author of Life	Acts 3:15	Quill
King of Kings	1 Timothy 6:15	Crown
Immanuel	Isaiah 7:14	"God with Us"
Lamb of God	John 1:29	Lamb
Light of the World	John 8:12	Candle
Lion of Judah	Revelation 5:5	Lion
The Good Shepherd	John 10:11	Staff
Alpha & Omega	Revelation 1:8	A and Ω
Bread of Life	John 6:35	Bread
Rock	1 Corinthians 10:4	Guitar
Judge of Israel	2 Timothy 4:1	Gavel
True Vine	John 15:1	Vine
Morning Star	Revelation 22:16	Rising Sun
Prince of Peace	Isaiah 9:6	Hand & Fingers
The Word	John 1:1-14	Scroll
Capstone	Psalm 118:22	Archway
Rose of Sharon	Song of Songs 2:1	Rose
Amen	Revelation 3:14	Praying Hands
Messiah	John 1:41	Cross
Resurrection and Life	John 11:25	Risen Lord

After I finished the stick, I began to study the results. Four of the titles come from the Old Testament, eighteen come from the New Testament. Nine different books are represented altogether. Over half are from the writings of John (ten from the Gospel of John, four from the book of Revelation). As a matter of fact, four titles come from the first chapter of John alone. I finished it in February 2011.

In March 2011, I
started working on the next
Bible Stick. I had been thinking
about this idea for some time. I got the idea
from a camp stick I carved in 2008. The camp stick
was carved with a spiral at the top. Another stick with a
matching spiral was carved to slide into the top. It looked like a
candy cane when in place.

Then I began to think, *I wonder if I could carve a third stick and slide it in the opposite direction?*
I did not know if it had been done before. I did not know if it was possible. I looked everywhere
on the internet but could not find this pattern anywhere.

That is when I decided, just try it. I went to the Midwest Dowel Shop and bought three dowel rods: walnut,
cherry, and poplar. I knew those three types of woods would look nice together. But before I carve a full-
length Bible Stick, I need to experiment with a smaller piece. So I carved a 1-foot sample piece. It worked!

Now I am ready to begin carving the full length Bible Stick. I first carve the poplar (white in color) and
the cherry (red in color). To do that, I mark the sticks, then take masking tape and cover them in a spiral.
The exposed wood is what I carve away. When finished, they slide together.

It took me about a year to carve the poplar and cherry. After I finished that step, I was ready to go to the next phase, carving the walnut (dark brown in color). I mask it off, and it is ready to carve.

I would carve both at the same time, constantly checking to make sure everything lined up perfectly. I took me about six months to carve the walnut, matching it with the cherry/poplar stick.

The final step was to decide on a Bible theme. The most logical idea was to go with the Trinity since I had called this pattern the Trinity pattern. But I did not know how to do it. I wrestled with many ideas but did not like any of them.

It finally came to me, instead of the title being at the top of the stick (which is how I have carved every other Bible Stick), I would carve the title into the walnut, and it would stretch the entire length of the stick. The title would say, *"THE HOLY TRINITY: GOD THE FATHER, GOD THE SON, GOD THE HOLY SPIRIT."* I painted the letters gold to make them stand out against the dark brown walnut.

Then in the checkered areas (the cherry and poplar), I would list all of the Bible passages that talked about the Trinity.

The first part is labeled, *THE NATURE OF THE TRINITY.* I have five Bible passages listed that refer to the Godhead, the three in one. I wanted to use both Old Testament and New Testament passages. The five passages are:

Genesis 1:26 - Then God said, "Let us make man in our image, in our likeness."

Matthew 28:19 – Therefore go and make disciples of all nations, baptizing them in the name of the Father and of the Son and of the Holy Spirit.

1 Peter 1:2 – Who have been chosen according to the foreknowledge of God the Father, through the sanctifying work of the Spirit, for obedience to Jesus Christ and sprinkling by his blood.

2 Corinthians 13:14 – May the grace of the Lord Jesus Christ, and the love of God, and the fellowship of the Holy Spirit be with you all.

1 Corinthians 12:4-6 – There are different kinds of gifts, but the same Spirit. There are different kinds of service, but the same Lord. There are different kinds of working, but the same God works all of them in all men.

From there, I then focus on the different roles of the Godhead. I wanted to use similar terms for each role. So each role has two words, the first word ending in "ing," the second word ending in "or." Plus I have several passages supporting those roles.

Role of the Father: RULING CREATOR

Psalm 103:19 – The Lord has established his throne in heaven, and his kingdom rules over all.

Genesis 1:1 – In the beginning God created the heavens and the earth.

1 Corinthians 8:6 – Yet for us there is but one God, the Father, from whom all things came and for whom we live.

Role of the Son: REDEEMING SAVIOR

John 3:16-17 – For God so loved the world that he gave his one and only Son, that whoever believes in him shall not perish but have eternal life. For God did not send his Son into the world to condemn the world, but to save the world through him.

1 John 5:11 – And this is the testimony: God has given us eternal life, and this life is in his Son.

Romans 6:23 – For the wages of sin is death, but the gift of God is eternal life in Christ Jesus our Lord.

Role of the Holy Spirit: INDWELLING COUNSELOR

John 16:7-8 – But I tell you the truth: It is for your good that I am going away. Unless I go away, the Counselor will not come to you; but if I go, I will send him to you. When he comes, he will convict the world of guilt in regard to sin and righteousness and judgment.

1 Corinthians 3:16 – Don't you know that you yourselves are God's temple and that God's Spirit lives in you?

1 Corinthians 12:4 – There are different kinds of gifts, but the same Spirit.

Acts 2:38 – Peter replied, "Repent and be baptized, every one of you, in the name of Jesus Christ for the forgiveness of your sins. And you will receive the gift of the Holy Spirit."

I did not want to use too many images on this stick. The pattern is what draws attention to it. The stick is mainly carved with words. But I did choose three different symbols to separate the roles. The first is the Celtic Knot, which is a symbol for the Trinity. The second is the ICHTHUS Fish and Cross to represent Jesus Christ. The third is the Dove inside the Flame to represent the Holy Spirit. I finished the stick in November 2013. I guess it took me over 300 hours to complete this Bible Stick.

For several years, different people told me about a woodcarver's museum in Dover, Ohio: The Mooney Warther Museum. I finally had an opportunity to go visit the museum in 1995. What an amazing place! Mooney Warther was definitely the master woodcarver, known for his detailed carvings depicting the history of the train. Mr. Warther passed away in 1973, but his son runs the museum today. I took several of my Bible Sticks for his evaluation. One of the things he said that encouraged me the most was that most people don't start carving until they retire. I started at a much younger age, 30 years old to be exact. If I continue to work at it, I will develop quite a skill by the time I retire.

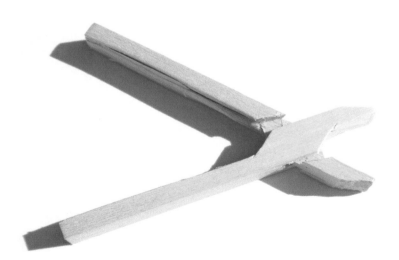

Mooney started carving wooden pliers when he was a boy. Take a piece of wood, put ten cuts in the wood, and they will open into a set of pliers. Mooney took this idea to the next level, carving several sets of pliers out of one piece of wood. He became nationally known for what he was able to do. His son, David Warther, carved a set of pliers for me. He showed me how to do it. I was fascinated with the idea.

Months later, I started trying it myself. I was able to carve a set after several tries. It then hit me (and again, this is one of the things for which I give credit to God), I could use the same principle, make a few adjustments, and carve a Cross with a moving cross bar. I began practicing with some balsa wood, a softer wood. I probably carved close to 200 crosses before I started carving them in bass wood, a harder wood. My practice resulted in carving one out of balsa wood in about 3 minutes, and about 10 minutes to carve one out of bass wood. I have taught several young men from my church how to carve the crosses. One of these days, they will be writing a book about what they have done.

I mentioned in the first chapter that the first stick I carved was a walking stick from my week of Wilderness Camp. I continue to be dean for that same week of camp. I have completed twenty-seven years. It has now become a tradition for me to carve a stick, including everyone's name. I always begin with my adult staff at the top of the list; then I put the kids' names on the stick, listing them in order of how many years they attended my week of camp.

Each camp stick is different. I will try new ideas I am experimenting with. I used dowel rods for my early years of carving, but recently, I have been carving from natural wood. My first camp stick had eleven names. Recently, I have had over forty-five names on each stick. I will carve the title a week before camp, but the names will be carved during the actual week.

Many people have asked if I have done anything besides woodcarving. I mentioned that I have a twin brother, Jon, and we grew up on a farm. One day when we were about 10 years old, we were exploring one of the big old barns on the farm. We found an old milk can in the barn. We took it home, cleaned it up, and painted it black. We decided to fill that thing with pennies! Well, I still have that milk can today, and I continue to fill it with pennies.

One day, it hit me. I could wallpaper an entire wall in my home with all these pennies. The more I thought about it, the more I realized that I could put in different designs because new pennies are bright and shiny, and old pennies are dark and brown. I could make designs like hearts, squares, diamonds, circles, and crosses. I could also make a picture of a person using all the different shades in between. Well, I did not cover an entire wall, but I did make a picture of Jesus, all out of pennies.

It was not that difficult. I took a picture of Jesus I liked, made an overhead transparency, and shot the image up on the wall. Wherever it was dark, I put a dark penny; wherever it was light, I put a light penny. I used sticky tac to hang each penny on the wall. It is about 3 feet high, 2 ½ feet wide. Even I was surprised at the outcome. A total of 1,300 pennies were used. The youth group from Western Hills Church of Christ have helped me make thirteen penny pictures through the years, giving them as gifts to different missions and organizations.

I don't know what God has planned for the future. I am always asked questions like "What are you going to do with all of these Bible Sticks?" "What are you working on now?" "What are you going to do next?" "Do you sell them?"

I'm not sure what the future holds, but I do know that as long as I continue to show honor and glory to God in all that I do and I continue to do my very best for Him, He will bless it beyond anything I have ever imagined. It even says in Proverbs 16:3, "Commit to the Lord whatever you do, and your plans will succeed." That is the challenge I want to leave with you. Whatever you do, do something that will glorify God (Colossians 3:17) and do your very best because you are doing this for the Lord, not for man. The Lord deserves our very best (Colossians 3:23). May God bless you in all that you do.

Printed in the United States
by Baker & Taylor Publisher Services